Choynika

Chelsea Hossain

BookLeaf Publishing

India | USA | UK

Presentation by *BookLeaf Publishing*

Web: www.bookleafpub.com

E-mail: info@bookleafpub.com

ISBN: 9789360948498

First edition 2024

I dedicate this book to Shane. Thank you for inspiring me. I love you. ~~for making a dreamer's dream come true~~.

Creation

Alone in another plane of mind.
The known and unknown combine.
Thoughts, formed, now surface
Each moment created, sublime.

So full of pride
and at a point
in life, where I am
young, but considered
an adult. I tried my best
to hide, the lack of
experience on my
side. And then my
anger takes hold
when I am told by the old,
you are young and
confused. Trapped by the
past and the future too
removed by the present
which keeps you young
and healthy. The future
is too daunting. To think
one day you'll lose, all
that that keeps you
amused. Parties and
alcohol. Living life
like eternal ones.
Never thinking it will
end. They say enjoy
it while you can. As the

hourglass upturned
loses its sand. Time
will reveal itself to you.
If you are worried
you are walking
through, your life
unaware of who
you are inside.

The Gilded Cage

The birdcage hung high and bold,
touched by King Midas, it turned gold.
The midday sun caught the cage
and shimmered, strangers would stop
to look and snicker, if only I was a little richer!
No one noticed the bluebird within.
No one paid the price for Midas' sin.
Freedom from greed is her only desire.
But no one could ever start that fire.
Wings clipped, her soul ripped from her life.
She was content to watch other's strife.

Lachrymose

The girl with a stone heart
Shed no tears from her eyes
She resisted love in every part
from those who actually tried.
Hatred from isolation took over
She told everyone pretty lies.
I do not need anyone.
My need for freedom is why.

As she walked down memory lane
She remembered life as full of wonder
Every rosebush and its thorns of pain
was an adventure she had blundered.
As time and pain wore on,
age and experience grew strong.
She moved on to the next chapter.

The constant isolation was caused
by her family who were driven by fear.
They wanted no influences here.
Wooden sticks and machetes
Disciplinary acts performed, forgetting
religion and values in exchange
for their own need for a target
of their own anger and pain.

She was a seeker of truth not ease
Penguin-suited women, the epitome
Of hypocrisy, of misogyny, of ascendancy.
Closed-minded fools seeking familiarity
Through generations of ritual tradition
Not actual belief.

Wrinkles and wisdom took their course
Day after day she became morose
Dark circles under her eyes, pronounced
And one by one she was denounced
For the existence of her mind outside the box.
Her ideas too threatening against the clock.

In her anguish, she still remained,
the breaker of cycles and bearer of pain
The stronger one among them as she tried
to see the world through another's eyes.

Her maudlin mind remembered she was
an empty page waiting to be written.

Free from the gilded cage she was within.
Open-hearted, open-minded soul.
A heart full of love it, never grew old.
Time tears youth and innocence away.

She is not who she once was.
She is not who she wishes to be.

She is stuck somewhere in-between.
She is lachrymose.

Know it All

Mouths hang open
as words of hatred spill out.
Jealousy begins dripping
from the drool that pools
on the ground. Though I
know where you come from and
know the void from which you speak
Your words are like knives.
Like a woodpecker's beak.
The noise you make is
incessant and your lack
becomes evident. Your
projection of shadows
is an image of self-detriment.

Freedom

She was trapped in her gloom
In a life she couldn't choose
For your safety they said
For your future
What is life without hard work and sacrifice?

Every night
She closed her eyes
But opened her mind

She felt her arms transform into wings
Blue feathers sprouting from the pores of her
skin
She felt her body get smaller and smaller
Her legs receding beneath her
She was at the windowsill
Claws clutching the edge
And looked out the window
At the vast expense of the night sky
And felt a tug in her gut
A longing for what could be
She spread her blue wings
And leaped

The air cushioned her fall

Ruffling her feathers
Her joy was unimaginable
Her beauty undiminished
Surfing with the waves of the wind
She maneuvered toward the places she had never
been
Knowing that she could never bring herself to
come back

Back to the life where her decisions were not her
own
Where mistakes are not condoned
Where life is a burden
Back to where everything is planned
Education, education, education
A tiring and constant routine
Back to where her focus is always on what she
needs
And her happiness is never guaranteed
Back to where she works for tomorrow
And suffers today
To where everyday another weight of stress and
unhappiness
On her shoulders
Keeping her from rising to her full potential

So she left every night
In her mind she was free
She can go where she pleased

She was independent and weightless
And she never wanted to come back

For the taste of freedom was much too sweet
The adrenaline was like a drug
She was addicted but never sorry

Those closest to her could never understand
Her heart's most desperate demand
To soar as high as the clouds
To reach for the sky
To be as free as a bird

Bluebird

On a drizzly, cloudy day
I gazed longingly at the heavens
My soul is so lost
My heart is full of questions.
Then suddenly, I saw a flash of blue as
My long-lost flying friend flew
Surfing the watery wind
Her damp wings gave in
Diving for her longing friend
Landing with so much grace
My heart was full of love as I stared at her face.
Perched on my shoulder, looking a little older
Her majestic blue wings folded back into place
Her head cocked toward the side of my face
Her small, black beaded eyes shone,
As she considered my silly form.
She was here for only one moment.
As we looked at each other
I looked in the mirror
The rain stopped its reign of terror.
She turned her tiny head away and
In one moment of movement
I felt the press of her weight
I knew it was time again to wait.
With sadness, I took in all her sweet particulars

Cherished the beauty of her beautiful blue
feathers
And just like that, her wings opened and took
flight
She floated, heavenly toward the light
As I watched, I felt weightlessness.

Crystal Clear

The diminishing moment,
when existing brings sorrow.
The pains of yesterday,
collide with tomorrow's.
The intentions of the blind
so out of place.
Preachers out of practice
Doubters out of faith.
The crystals of fear
holding your energy
a representation of
your deepest enemies.
Cloudy, swirling, swarms
of negativity, overtaking
your pure soul, in poverty.
Chasing temporary highs
in place of the lows.
Oh, how well you would do
if you just faced it all.
Opened your mind to it.
The voice within you
leading your soul to the
future of love. Following
your own moral compass.
Facing your fears, giving

back to the needy, weeding
out the people who do not
care about you truly. There
is a purpose for all the good
and the bad. Rise up from
the ground and turn your
crystals back into crystal clear
clarity.

Future Enticer

Within a circle of flames,
fire as high as the sky.
My soul awaits its name,
as an apocalyptic impending
end, beginning to portend
some semblance of sobriety
for the incoming calamity,
a foreboding death of mankind.

A collective mind will
be created to
face the future of the
human race. No one
super hero, alter ego
or prideful face can
save the space once
AI takes the place of
mankind. Not one
human will be equivalent
to its quantum mind.

All the humans will
embrace each other
As tragedy brings everyone
together. Will it be enough?

Can I forgive the corporations
who acted as God? To
"save the nation" through
the creation
of the silver-suited machines.
In the image
of human greed. We created
a life of ease
to live like
Kings and Queens on a throne
of skulls and bones of
peasants who bore their
way to the top
and dared
to open their mouths to the
future they knew would
come.
The people in power
scared little cowards,
kill off the prophets one
by one
with an army of
AI's by their side ending
all of their influence.
Tyrants and oppressors,
figments of futures lead to a
New World Order.

The universe is too big,
man too selfish
to see that we are not the
only living ones.
Nations and corporations
cooperating to supposedly "protect".
Taking our freedoms and
our free will to "save us" from
alien invasions with our own
creations of evil nuclear weapons
and AI monstrosities. The public
only know the story told
by the people in power who
control the chessboard. The truth
a secret we may never uncover
until it is too late.

We are all pawns
slaving away
supplying the money
for their game.
My only hope
is God's holy tropes in the
books of old that hold
the human moral code.

The White Mountain

Far from where I stand,
After miles of empty land,
A tall Mountain peeks
behind clouds and speaks,
as snow tumbles 'n pours,
the mighty mountain roars,
"I destroy your lives!
So that you may live!"

In Between

Thoughts born-now surface dancing.
Though they circle back, wistfully, to you
in your dark well, denying you languish.
With past and your present confused
Though the path you'd described calls for parting
still drawn, am I, to your love
My soul still calls out for your shaping
Mold my wings and I'll soar like a dove

Eye of the Storm

An eye of blue skies and a sunny day
Lies at the center of a stormy fate.
Within a swirling, swarming wind of hate
A spiral of destruction you create
In a moment of madness you deviate
From the calm, centered being that's innate

Heavenly Oceans

As the sun set beyond the horizon,
My eyes rose high to the blinding sun.
I stared out toward the waving water.
The tides shaping heaven's author.
I dug my cold toes in the sinking sand,
as my mind and body took its final stand.

My soul is as cold as the depths of the ocean.
My mind set on committing the evil deed.
I followed the example of Mother Nature,
the weakest among us will suffer and bleed.
Our Mother Gaia takes no survivors,
for all who are living are doomed to die.
But I guess I didn't learn her lesson.
She disciplines those with closed eyes.

I watched from the shores of the oceans,
as many moons and seasons pass.
The sun set beyond the horizon.
Every heavenly star on its own path.

You

Your eyes of pale blue,
take me someplace else.
I have seen the depth of your ocean.
I survived your wave of death.
The stormy grays of our love,
Will not break my voice,
Nor my faith.
But my own heart is guiding me,
Deeper into the abyss.

With my head above the water
My feet, nowhere near the ground.
I look at the heavens and
their weeping clouds.
This ocean they have created,
I have made it my own house.
A cold, calculated destruction by waves,
in line with the chaotic nature of the wind,
a perfect balance for committing a sin.
A breath of relief,
before the destruction begins.
An imitation of the darkness of chagrin.
Our swirling dance of water and wind.
Work well together for what we intend.
In the destruction of our lives,

Over one sin.

But I see you, at the eye of the storm
In that place, still,
lies your true form.
Your gentle spirit, your sweet, loving soul.
My weakness,
Formed your windy storms
The pain I caused became my own.
I claimed your heart,
and our hearts were torn,
by my ocean of tears,
navigating the unknown.

So to the Kingdom of God, I made my way.
I turned to Adam to hear him say,
respect of the divine is the only way.

Below the willow tree,
I choose to wait.
Show me my destiny.
I accept my fate.
Show me a sign.
Give me my sight,
and I promise,
I will open my eyes.

As I turned to face my man in fear,
I said the darkness exists nowhere but here.

He said, one moment it's there,
And then it's gone.
My heart beats for the beat of your drum.
From beginning to end.
For years to come,
I see us as one.

As I drowned in your eyes,
I saw my reflection.

Patience

I have seen a glimpse of the future.
I know the roots of that willow tree.
It spent most of its time waiting,
for its life to emerge from its seed.
Though my eyes want to water your garden,
I will close my gates up tight.
I will wait to show you my power.
Because all you need is time.
I will meet you where life is not a race.
Where you can run at your own pace.
I bestow upon you my understanding,
In hope you find your own place.

Now I Wait

The prescience
of what's to come,
is greater than fear
as I sit in the sun.
As I hold you beneath,
this deep-rooted tree.
Limbs like strong arms,
swaying, rainy leaves.
A breath-taking reminder
of a fresh, filtered breeze,
from lichen growing green,
the grass beneath my feet,
grounding, encapturing me,
beneath the sky, above the
Earth. Grown straight from,
the brown dirt.
Here, in the Now, I wait.

Evergreen

With every graceful step you take, nature sings.
Grass once down-trodden, suddenly springs.
Your pale-blue eyes touch the cloudless sky
And all at once, gray clouds gather to bring,
life back from the deep winter's cold sleep.

The bluebirds hear your beautiful cry and dive
Searching for the source of their nature and
pride.
They land on the strong boughs of your tree.
Nestle their small head upon your green leaves.
And the wind whistles your name, Evergreen.

Just Friends

Take me back to the time when,
your hand was in my hand.
And our bodies were entangled
like old-fangled particles.
Dancing in circles.
Colliding in communion.
Creating stars in our union.
You are the sunlight of my days.
I am the darkness of your nights.
We exist together at dawn and twilight.
With the rise of the sun, I see your face.
At the end of the day, you fade away.
Like two dancers grabbing hold
of each other, and then twirling away
day after day. An eternal dance of love.
Dancing to the music and the beat of the drum.
Along with nature's beautiful hum.
I could remain forever in your arms.

Godsend

At the stroke of dawn
Time slows down
I awake in wait
Of your response
To the never-ending
Dance of chance
One moment to the
Next unspoken
yet felt by the bond
Of two souls bound by
God.

Blue Moons

In the darkness of space,
planets form and die
affected by an embrace
or the wings of a butterfly.

Planets are formed by the
vision envisioned by God.
His will is reflected within and
between us.

You fear your blue moon is
caught by my gravity.
But we are both blue moons
circling planets in eternity.

I long for what lies on Orion's belt.
Like a fisherman fishing for kelt.
The hungry hunter's arrow aims,
in the constellation where you framed,
A dove chasing a bluebird, our game.

The hungry hunter may claim
he does not love the dove.
He says he is after the chase.
To fill a void emptier than space.

But order and chaos are linked
Like blue moons caught in gravity
Like Orion's blue-eyed wink
As the planets and stars form and fall
It creates certain realities.

Field of Flowers

I have a never-ending hunger for
The trunk of your tree.
Limbs bowing next to me
Using your boughs to dance with me
As spring sprouts and raises
Flowers and trees in places
Of desolation of natural beauty
Cherry blossoms and pollen fly
freely, as I lay in the green grass
among my field of flowers.
As all things reproduce.
All things must choose.
And have already chosen.
Like roses that grow in bushes
and rivers that flow interconnected.
And thus I explain, my love
I need what I want and
I want what I desire.
My roots are wet but you start a fire
All consuming my mind as I lay
entangled in your grape vines
From which I create sweet wine
That I drink to have you inside.
A burning passion I can't hide.
I am this open field of flowers
You are my beehive.

www.ingramcontent.com/pod-product-compliance
Lightning Source LLC
La Vergne TN
LVHW010949200726